COME, TAKE UP YOUR CROSS

The Practical Responsibilities of Christians Today

FLANN LYNCH, O.F.M., Cap.

Ave Maria Press • Notre Dame, Indiana 46556

Nihil Obstat:
     Brendan E. O'Mahoney, O.F.M. Cap.
     Provincial
Imprimatur:
     ✠John Mackey, D.D.
     Auckland, New Zealand

Library of Congress Catalog Card Number: 77-608263
International Standard Book Number: 0-87793-144-5

First published in 1976 by The Word Publishers Ltd., Auckland, New Zealand.
Published in 1978 in the United States of America by Ave Maria Press, Notre Dame, Indiana 46556.

Photography: Michael Tubberty
Design and typography: Cae Esworthy

Printed and bound in the United States of America.

Contents

FOREWORD

The command of the Lord to all he calls to himself to be his people is "Be holy, because I the Lord, Your God, am holy."

God manifested his holiness first in the commands of the Old Testament and finally in the commands and the person of Christ in the New Testament.

Our holiness consists in putting on Christ, having the same mind that was in Christ, growing up to maturity in Christ. These are all phrases of St. Paul that express how we become holy.

Mother Church has a long tradition of breaking these general phrases of St. Paul into operational definitions that were called the spiritual and the corporal works of mercy.

This present book by Father Flann Lynch, O.F.M. Cap., has taken the substance of these ideas and framed them into meditations pointed to present circumstances. If you would be holy as your heavenly Father is holy, you may find great profit in these prayerful meditations.

†John Mackey
Bishop of Auckland

INTRODUCTION

Confusion, uncertainty and anxiety have haunted many
Catholics since the Second Vatican Council. Happily, the
Church now seems to have arrived at a position of greater
stability. This is not to say that we can feel free to subside
into a comfortable Christianity. Renewal is a constant task
for every person and renewal means that we accept the
responsibility to keep on changing for the better. The word
"change" expresses well the active role of true Christian
living. To quote Cardinal Newman: "To live is to change; to
be perfect is to have changed often." In trying to be faithful
to our Christian responsibilities, we bring about this change
in ourselves and in others.

This book of meditations is an attempt to outline the
responsibilities of a Christian in the chief areas of human life
—what used to be called the corporal and spiritual works of
mercy. Christian responsibility has its source in God's own
word and that is why I have begun each meditation with

selected passages from Sacred Scripture. I have linked up the meditations with the Stations of the Cross to try to show that Jesus is still on the way to Calvary, still suffering in our deprived and needy brothers and sisters.

The book may be of use to families, groups, parish councils, or it may be used for personal prayer and reflection. Committees could allocate 30 minutes at the beginning of meetings for prayerful study. This study could begin with the prayer and the reading of the scripture passages, followed by a short period of silence. The reflection could then be read and discussed with the help of the questions in the response. If a group is to get maximum benefit, the individual members will obviously need to prepare beforehand the section to be covered.

There are also other possible ways in which the book could be used. Where time is limited, as in a family situation, a scripture passage could be read, followed by a brief silence to consider the work of mercy and the suffering of Jesus, concluding with the prayer.

Father Flann Lynch, O.F.M. Cap.

Jesus Is Condemned to Death

PRAYER

Lord Jesus, you had great compassion for the hungry.
You performed an astonishing miracle to provide food for
the hungry.
You accepted the sentence of death out of love for the
hungry.
Forgive us for condemning you to death in those that die of
starvation.
Lord, already we deserve your words of condemnation,
"I was hungry and you did not feed me. Away from me.
I do not know you."
Who shall climb the mountain of the Lord?
Who shall stand in his holy place?
The man with clean hands and pure heart, who desires not,
nor covets riches or material possessions to the neglect
of aiming at the higher life and its superior values.
Dear Jesus, help us to revolutionize our thinking.
Make us like you, willing to deny ourselves, willing to suffer
out of love for the hungry.
Give us the spirit of the early Christians.
Help us not to make a god of our possessions but to give
generously of ourselves.

Ann **1.** Jesus is condemned to death

Carol

SHARE YOUR RESOURCES

Jesus is full of compassion for the hungry.

Jesus called his disciples to him and said, "I feel sorry for all the people; they have been with me for three days now and have nothing to eat. I do not want to send them off hungry, they might collapse on the way." The disciples said to him, "Where could we get enough bread in this deserted place to feed such a crowd?" Jesus said to them, "How many loaves have you?" "Seven," they said, "and a few small fish." Then he instructed the crowd to sit down on the ground, and he took the seven loaves and the fish and he gave thanks and broke them and handed them to the disciples who gave them to the crowds. They all ate as much as they wanted, and they collected what was left over of the scraps, seven baskets full. Now four thousand men had eaten, to say nothing of women and children.

Matthew 15:32-38

The early Christian community shared what they had with the hungry.

Carol

The whole group of believers was united heart and soul; no one claimed for his own anything he had, as everything they owned was held in common. There was a Levite of Cypriot origin called Joseph surnamed Barnabas (which means "son of encouragement"). He owned a piece of land and he sold it and brought the money, and presented it to the apostles.

Acts 4:32, 36-37

Christians today allow the hungry to die.

"For I was hungry and you never gave me food."

Matthew 25:42

REFLECTION

The example of Jesus and the early Christians shows that religion is a matter of love and self-sacrifice. We can reduce religion to an insurance policy that we hope will protect us against the worst the future might bring. We pay the premium by doing little things for God, saying little prayers, giving a little money for the hungry of the world. In this way we bargain with God, making religion so much less than the loving relationship God wants it to be.

In a materialist age we are highly prone to slip into an apathetic attitude which ignores the life and death struggle of our fellowman. If we are prepared to spend large amounts of money on luxuries, color TV, power boats, expensive holidays, does not Jesus expect us to donate as

11

much to the hungry? We do not always realize how much more rewarding it is to give to the needy and desperate . . . that they live! Parishes should harness the energies of the community to:

(a) Determine wants and needs
(b) Organize the purchase and dispatch of such needs
(c) Reassess or reappraise parish energy potential
(d) Put into action the adoption responsibility for a given area, church or city in needy countries

Mother Teresa, speaking to pilgrims at the Eucharistic Congress in Philadelphia made the following request: "I ask you one thing, never be afraid of giving, but don't give from your abundance, give until it hurts."

RESPONSE

1. How do we differ from Jesus and from the early Christians?
2. Is it reasonable to expect us to cut down on what we spend on luxuries, pleasures, entertainment, or to fast sometimes, giving the money saved to the hungry?
3. What connection is there between our overindulgence and the poverty and starvation of others?

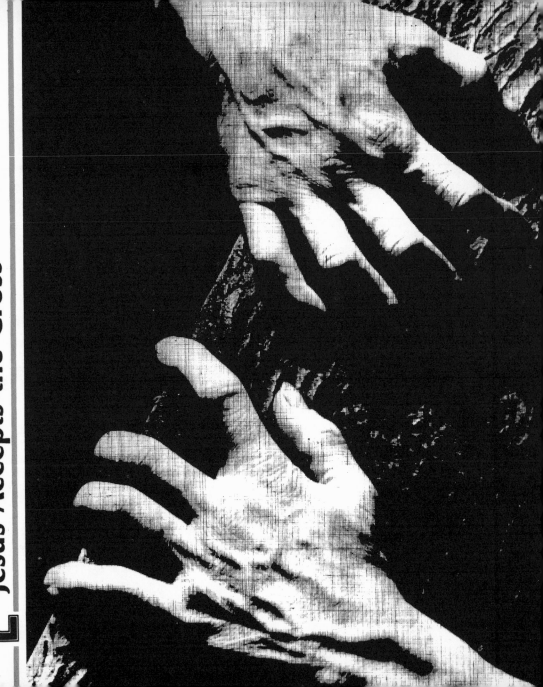

2 Jesus Accepts the Cross

PRAYER

Lord Jesus, our good deeds and our religious practices can
be selfishly geared toward our own salvation.
Fill our hearts with hunger and thirst for justice.
Lord, we recognize our guilt in the rich man, for we crucify
you again and again in the hungry and the thirsty.
Forgive us our gross overindulgence that keeps the poor, the
Lazaruses of the world, in shocking suffering, misery and
degradation.
We see you, Lord, hanging from the cross and crying out in
agony, "I thirst."
Help us to hear your cries by giving financial support and by
urging governments to give more aid.
As you were given vinegar and gall to drink, help us to deny
ourselves the luxury of favorite drinks.
Dear Jesus, help us to give generously as the widow gave
her mite. Fill our hearts with hunger
and thirst for justice.

15

Jesus accepts
the cross

Carol

GIVE TO THE NEEDY

Carol

**Jesus gives his life. How much does he expect us to give?
The widow gives everything. How much do we give?**

Jesus sat down opposite the treasury and watched the
people putting money into the treasury and many of the rich
put in a great deal. A poor widow came and put in two
small coins, the equivalent of a penny. Then he called his
disciples and said to them, "I tell you solemnly, this poor
widow has put more in than all who have contributed to the
treasury; for they have all put in money they had over, but
she from the little she had put in everything she possessed, all
she had to live on."

Mark 12:41-44

Do we differ from the rich man in the following parable?

"There was a rich man who used to dress in purple and fine
linen and feast magnificently every day. And at his gate
there lay a poor man called Lazarus, covered with sores,

16

who longed to fill himself with the scraps that fell from the rich man's table. Dogs even came and licked his sores. Now the poor man died and was carried away by the angels to the bosom of Abraham. The rich man also died and was buried. In his torment in Hades he looked up and saw Abraham a long way off with Lazarus in his bosom. So he cried out, "Father Abraham, pity me and send Lazarus to dip the tip of his finger in water and cool my tongue, for I am in agony in these flames." "My son," Abraham replied, "remember that during your life good things came your way, just as bad things came the way of Lazarus. Now he is being comforted here while you are in agony. But that is not all: between us and you a great gulf has been fixed, to stop anyone, if he wanted to, crossing from our side to yours, and to stop any crossing from your side to ours."

Luke 16:19-26

God rewards the generous giver with his favor and blessings.

Do not forget: thin sowing means thin reaping; the more you sow, the more you reap. Each one should give what he has decided in his own mind, not grudgingly or because he is made to, for God loves a cheerful giver. And there is no limit to the blessings God can send you—he will make sure you will always have all you need for yourselves in every possible circumstance, and still have something to spare for all sorts of good works. As scripture says: He was free in almsgiving and gave to the poor: his good deeds will never be forgotten.

2 Corinthians 9:6-9

REFLECTION

The Christian vision of life that sees humanity living in peace and harmony is still a dream. Struggle for money, greed for monopoly and power keep more than two-thirds of the world in poverty and hardship. In the parable of the rich man and poor Lazarus, Jesus tells how the baptized rich persons who fail to give to the poor are rejected by their Lord, while he receives with open arms the victims of exploitation. We are the rich men, the exploiters, for we belong to that one-fifth of humanity that consumes 85 per cent of the world's wealth; 90 per cent of its energy and fuel and 80 per cent of its protein. We spend colossal amounts of money on spirits, beer, wine and soft drinks while two-thirds of the world rarely if ever enjoy the luxuries of milk, tea or coffee. We enjoy every material consolation and spiritual ones too, such as the gift of sacramental life, the privilege of prayer and the promise of eternal life.

The story of Lazarus together with the millions that are dying of starvation is a serious warning and should trouble our consciences. Only altered attitudes can put our minds at ease.

We must opt out of "keeping up with the Jones's" and direct our attention to the needy. We must refuse to see life as having meaning only if there is a rise in living standards. Justice for people everywhere must replace our selfish obsession with greater comfort. Justice means treating distress by putting food and drink in the mouth of those who starve. But justice also demands that we treat the causes of distress. This mostly means helping people to help themselves.

Over two-thirds of the world's population live in subhuman conditions and the number is increasing. Yet governments are reducing aid when they should be increasing it. "Open your mouth for the dumb" is God's command to us in the Book of Proverbs. These words tell us to be a lobby for those who have no voice. Political involvement therefore becomes imperative to ensure that all political parties give priority to development programs and to force governments to give a greater percentage of the gross national product for aid. We can also help people to help themselves by urging governments to send a percentage of those who want to enter the armed forces to do a term of volunteer service in a developing country. Volunteer services ought also to be organized and financed (if necessary) at parish level.

Archbishop Helder Camara of Brazil states that "we Christians need to get closer to all those who believe that we all have the same Father and, therefore, are brothers. Without resorting to violence we should unite ourselves to demand justice. The poor and the oppressed are Christ himself and the great charity of our time consists in helping to promote justice."

RESPONSE

1. How do we differ from the rich man in the above parable?
2. How much time should we keep for ourselves?
3. How much time should we spend working for justice?

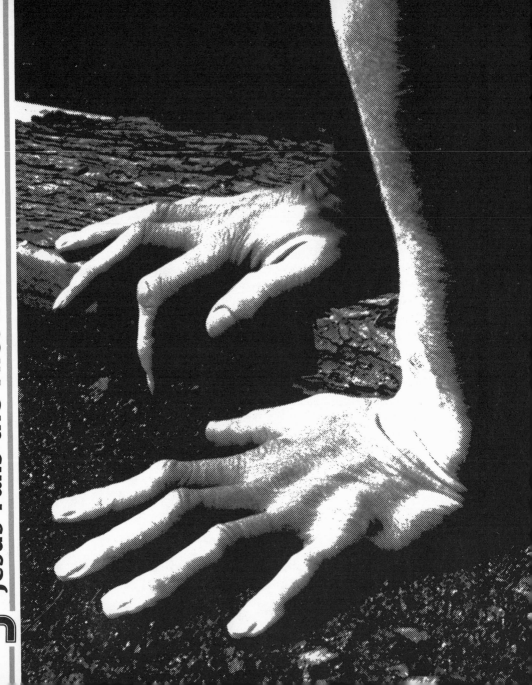

3 Jesus Falls the First Time

PRAYER

Lord Jesus, you are almighty Lord, the giver of all good
    things.

Thank you for your goodness in giving us the necessities of
    life.

Forgive us if we are too concerned with our own security, or
    if we are greedy for material things.

Give us greater faith and trust in your goodness.

Help us to live more simply and to appreciate the best things
    in life, the things that money cannot buy.

Help us to regard our faith as the pearl beyond price.

Help us to say with Paul: "For me to live is Christ."

Dear Jesus, in great agony you fall under the weight of the
    cross.

Your agony continues in those who lack the bare necessities
    of life.

Help us to recognize you in the poor and to give what we
    can afford to alleviate your suffering.

LIVE MORE SIMPLY

Jesus questions the depth of our faith, warns us against greed and commands that we live simply.

"No one can be the slave of two masters: he will either hate the first and love the second, or treat the first with respect and the second with scorn. You cannot be the slave both of God and of money. That is why I am telling you not to worry about your life and what you are to eat, nor about your body and how you are to clothe it. Surely life means more than food and the body more than clothing. Look at the birds of the sky. They do not sow or reap or gather into barns; yet your heavenly Father feeds them. Are you not worth much more than they are? Can any of you, for all his worrying, add one single cubit to his span of life? And why worry about clothing? Think of the flowers growing in the fields; they never have to work or spin, yet I assure you that not even Solomon in all his regalia was robed like one of these. Now if that is how God clothes the grass in the field which is there today and thrown into the furnace tomorrow, will he not much more look after you, you men of little faith? So do not worry; do not say, "What are we to eat? What are we to drink? How are we to be clothed?" It is the pagans who set their hearts on all these things. Your heavenly Father knows you need them all. Set your hearts on his kingdom first and on his righteousness, and all these other things will be given you as well. So do not worry about tomorrow; tomorrow will take care of itself. Each day has enough trouble of its own."

Matthew 6:24-34

Jesus does not recommend giving; he commands it!

Carol

"Sell your possessions and give alms. Get yourselves purses that do not wear out, treasure that will not fail you, in heaven where no thief can reach it and no moth destroy it. For where your treasure is there will your heart be also."

Luke 12:33-34

REFLECTION

St. Paul took Jesus at his word in the above passage. "For me to live is Christ," he said. Though he earned his living as a tentmaker, Paul got his basic security and satisfaction from his faith in Jesus.

We do not accept fully what Jesus says to us in the first reading and so we cannot say with full sincerity: "for me to live is Christ!" We make material comforts and status symbols sources of security and objects of affection. And so, very often when we say "I love you" to God or to people,

23

we mean it with an enormous I and a tiny you. What we really love are our status symbols—good clothes, good car, modern home, prestige in the community.

This way of life promotes selfishness, brings only superficial and short-lived satisfaction and causes us to lose sight of the hardships of those in need. Little wonder, then, that our Lord places so much emphasis on the importance of simple living.

The right to private property is not an absolute right. Jesus tells us that if we have two coats we must give one to him who has none. St. Ambrose tells us: "You are not making a gift of your possessions to the poor person. You are handing over to him what is his. For what has been given in common for the use of all you have arrogated to yourself. The world is given to all and not only to the rich." St. Basil is equally forthright. "The garment hanging in your wardrobe is the garment of him who is naked. The shoes you do not wear are the shoes of the one who is barefoot. The money you keep locked away is the money of the poor."

We give in dollars to the poor but if we are to escape God's anger and become truly Christian then we shall have to give in hundreds or even thousands, as well as giving of our time.

Christ does not expect us to become destitute but he expects us to give according to our means. The vast majority give far less than their means allow. A change of attitude, a revision of our order of values can come about only by deepening our faith, rethinking our faith and discovering its implications for, perhaps, the first time.

RESPONSE

1. Is being well dressed an important priority to us?
2. Why does Jesus lay such emphasis on the importance of simple living?
3. Should we take advantage of opportunities to buy clothes for those in need, if we can afford it?
4. Have we clothes that we rarely wear that others would be glad to have?

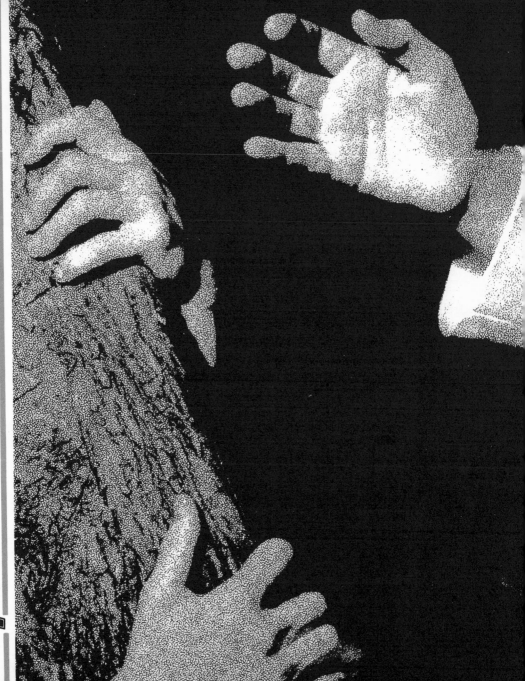

4 Jesus Meets His Mother

PRAYER

O Mary, our Mother, help us to count our blessings and be
truly grateful

Help us to realize how entirely dependent on God we are
for everything.

Help us to be truly grateful for the many signs of God's love.

Help us to be truly grateful for the way your divine Son
suffered for us.

Give us a compassionate heart to express our gratitude.

Help us to feel what you felt on the way to Calvary as we
meet your suffering Son in the imprisoned and in the
neglected.

Your Son wants us to visit and befriend him in the imprisoned
and in the underprivileged.

He wants us to combat the causes of crime and delinquency.

Intercede with your Son for us, that we may be generous with
our time, and not deserve his condemnation: "I was in
prison and you never visited me."

Lord Jesus, through the intercession of your holy Mother send
us the Holy Spirit that our hearts may be full of love and
compassion for the imprisoned, the delinquent, the
deprived and the neglected.

VISIT THE IMPRISONED

Carol

Three times Peter denied any knowledge of Jesus. Peter was happy to be a friend of Jesus before his arrest but not afterwards. We can be like Peter, rejecting people when they lose "respectability" through a prison sentence.

Peter, however, repented. Repentance for us would mean greater compassion for the imprisoned, expressed through our friendship and other practical ways.

Meanwhile Peter was siting outside in the courtyard, and a servant girl came up to him and said, "You too were with Jesus, the Galilean." But he denied it in front of them all. "I do not know what you are talking about," he said. When he went out to the gateway another servant girl saw him and said to the people there, "This man was with Jesus the Nazarene." And again, with an oath, he denied it, "I do not know the man." A little later the bystanders came up and said to Peter, "You are one of them for sure! Why, your accent gives you away." Then he started calling down curses on himself and swearing, "I do not know the man." At that moment the cock crew, and Peter remembered what Jesus had said, "Before the cock crows you will have disowned me three times." And he went outside and wept bitterly.

Matthew 26:69-75

God answered the prayers of the Christians for Peter's release. Prisoners have great need of our prayers for their well-being.

28

It was about this time King Herod started persecuting certain members of the Church. He beheaded James, the brother of John, and when he saw that this pleased the Jews, he decided to arrest Peter as well. This was during the days of Unleavened Bread, and he put Peter in prison, assigning four squads of four soldiers each to guard him in turns. Herod meant to try Peter after the end of Passover week. All the time Peter was under guard the Church prayed to God for him unremittingly. On the night before Herod was to try him, Peter was sleeping between two soldiers, fastened with double chains, while guards kept watch at the main entrance to the prison. Then suddenly the angel of the Lord stood there, and the cell was filled with light. He tapped Peter on the side and woke him up. "Get up!" he said, "Hurry"— and the chains fell from his hands.

Acts 12:1-7

We see in Acts how the apostles were imprisoned on a number of occasions. This time they rejoiced after having been flogged because they were found worthy to suffer like Christ. The apostles were able to do this because they had special graces, but the support and prayers of the Christian community were of great importance also.

Imprisonment is a chastening experience and can have a transforming effect on a person, leading to social reform and rehabilitation. This change is brought about by God's grace, our prayers and strong social activity in visiting prisons.

They had the apostles called in, gave orders for them to be flogged, warned them not to speak in the name of Jesus and released them. And so they left the presence of the Sanhedrin glad to have had the honor of suffering humiliation for the sake of the name.

Acts 5:40-41

REFLECTION

Pope John, soon after he became pope, made world headlines by visiting the prisoners in Regina Coeli prison in Rome. His gesture brought to our attention a forgotten and even despised section of the community. What is our attitude to the imprisoned? The term "jailbird" conveys a meaning which is less than human. Unconsciously we look on the inmates of prisons as the most despised form of human life, without dignity, without self-respect and without respect in the eyes of the community. Implicit in this attitude is a judgment on our part: "It serves him right. He doesn't deserve sympathy. He got off too lightly."

Pope John's visit to the prisoners was a reproach to our un-Christian attitude. We can judge quickly and harshly without taking the facts of a situation into account. We are all products of our upbringing and environment and with the same background we too might be criminals. "There but for the grace of God go you or I." Consequently Jesus tells us, "Judge not."

The words of scripture, "Despised, a worm, and no man," which describe the condition of Jesus on his way to Calvary, describe too the condition of people in prisons. Jesus (who was also a prisoner) still suffers in these people. He still needs visiting. We must be a "mother" to him.

Why do people go to prison? Who is responsible? Society helps create the conditions which breed delinquency. We are society. We are responsible. We can do much to offset the causes of delinquency. Every parish needs an active social services organization of voluntary helpers. Some full-time workers could seek out those in need and offer them support and help.

Every Catholic should feel responsible for his immediate neighborhood by extending hospitality and friendship to the needy and the neglected. Our failure to show this kind of active concern causes many people to end up in prison. Ex-prisoners, too, need our support and friendship if they are to rehabilitate themselves and become responsible citizens. The human race is one family. We are our brothers' keepers.

RESPONSE

1. Do we ever give a thought to prisoners?
2. Do we ever visit people in prison?
3. Do we feel any responsibility toward prisoners?
4. Can we take any practical steps to eliminate the causes of delinquency, or to rehabilitate prisoners or ex-prisoners?

Ann

PRAYER

Forgive us, Lord, if we are like the rich man.
Give us a change of heart while there is still time.
Give us a loving heart, a giving heart, that will blot out our
    many sins of greed and selfishness.
Dear Jesus, you had nowhere to lay your head.
Thank you for the security and shelter of a home.
We see Simon helping you to carry your cross, Lord,
And we think, "how natural, how fortunate he was to have
    had that opportunity."
Open our eyes, Lord, to the opportunities that present
    themselves each day.
Help us to be generous like Simon.
Help us to recognize our kinship with the poor and our
    responsibility toward them.
Help us to go to your aid as we find you in agony in the
    needy and the homeless.
Help us to give freely of our time, our hospitality and our
    possessions.

Carol

OFFER HOSPITALITY

Only the fool puts trust in material riches.

Jesus said to them, "Watch and be on your guard against avarice of any kind, for a man's life is not made secure by what he owns, even when he has more than he needs."

Then he told them a parable: "There was once a rich man who having a good harvest from his land thought to himself, 'What am I to do? I have not enough room to store my crops.' Then he said, 'This is what I will do: I will pull down my barns and build bigger ones, and store up all my grain and any goods in them and I will say to my soul: My soul, you have plenty of good things laid by for many years to come; take things easy, eat, drink, have a good time.' But God said to him: 'Fool, this very night the demand will be made for your soul; and this hoard of yours, whose will it be then?' So it is when a man stores up treasure for himself in place of making himself rich in the sight of God."

Luke 12:15-21

The follower of Jesus must be free from obsession with material things. If we are truly sincere Christians we must concern ourselves with the sufferings and hardships of less fortunate people.

One of the scribes then came up and said to him, "Master, I will follow you wherever you go." Jesus replied, "Foxes have holes and the birds of the air have nests, but the Son of Man has nowhere to lay his head."

Matthew 8:19-20

Those who receive Jesus in the Eucharist are looked on as one.

The bread that we break is a communion with the body of Christ. The fact that there is only one loaf means that, though there are many of us, we form a single body, because we all have a share in this one loaf.

1 Corinthians 10:16-17

REFLECTION

"Never a borrower or a lender be" is not a Christian maxim. Even the Old Testament commands mercy in this regard: "The just man takes pity and lends." The parable of the rich man shows the insanity of hoarding surplus money and possessions. Our generosity or lack of it is the standard by which we are judged: "I was homeless and you did, or did not, give me shelter."

Baptism unites us all as one in Jesus Christ and makes us responsible also for the unbaptized. This spiritual union,

35

which is stronger and deeper than blood relationships, is further strengthened by the Eucharist. This is a "disturbing" doctrine. Greed, selfishness, love of ease and comfort do not allow us even to consider its implications. Jesus, however, is so explicit that we cannot avoid the truth and its consequences. "I am the vine, you are the branches," which is to say we are all united in one intimate family, irrespective of race, geographical remoteness or other differences. Every time we receive the Eucharist we acknowledge our oneness with the poor and the homeless. The gift of the Eucharist also places upon us the responsibility of feeling and caring for all men as Jesus did. So the Eucharist makes us one with the suffering Jesus, helped by Simon, and still on the way to Calvary in those who lack the necessities of life. The Eucharist therefore places a most serious responsibility on us to go to the aid of Jesus as we find him homeless, in developing countries.

The local community, too, has many needs. Inadequate housing and lack of money can place great strains on family relationships. Because we do not care, people can become so desperate as to obtain abortions. There are many ways in which we can help. Be interested enough to get to know of people in need. Help them financially and if possible through friendship. Have we the luxury of summer residences when families are in desperate need of housing? The Catholics in a parish should pool together to provide housing for deserving people. Help families to make homes more habitable or help them with a necessary addition to the home. Be hospitable, have an open door, welcome people. When we do all this Jesus tells us to say, "We are ordinary servants; we have only done our duty."

RESPONSE

1. Are we friendly to our neighbors, especially those in need?
2. Should we be willing to look after a homeless child?
3. Should we be willing to contribute to a fund to provide housing, rent, etc., for the needy?
4. Why not start such a fund?

6 Veronica Wipes the Face of Jesus

PRAYER

Lord Jesus, we see Veronica wiping your bloody face and we
   think, how beautiful!
You are still with us Lord, still suffering in the sick.
Help us to be concerned enough to wipe your face with our
   compassion toward those in pain and suffering.
Touch our hearts with the example of your suffering and
   death.
Help us to reflect deeply on the parable of the Good
   Samaritan, and then to be good Samaritans wherever
   we find you in pain and suffering.
Lord, we are weak and selfish and it is hard for us to be
   good Samaritans.
Give us courage and strength.
Make us self-sacrificing like Veronica.
Make us generous with our time in visiting the sick.
Send the Holy Spirit to fill our hearts with compassion for the
   sick and the suffering that we may deserve to hear your
   words, "I was sick and you visited me."

Ann

6 . Veronica wipes the face of Jesus

Carol

VISIT THE SICK

Jesus has great compassion and love for the sick.

He went round the whole of Galilee teaching in their
synagogues, proclaiming the Good News of the kingdom
and curing all kinds of diseases and sickness among the
people. His fame spread throughout Syria, and those who
were suffering from diseases and painful complaints of one
kind or another, the possessed, epileptics, the paralyzed,
were all brought to him, and he cured them.

Matthew 4:23-24

**The message of the following reading is unmistakably clear.
"Get off the fence," Jesus tells us. "Get to work and don't
count the cost. Let the Veronica in you emerge to comfort
me in the sick."**

Carol

The man was anxious to justify himself and said to Jesus,
"And who is my neighbor?" Jesus replied, "A man was once
on his way down from Jerusalem to Jericho and fell into the

40

hands of brigands. They took all he had, beat him and then made off, leaving him half dead. Now a priest happened to be traveling down the same road, but when he saw the man, he passed by on the other side. In the same way a Levite who came to the place saw him, and passed by on the other side. But a Samaritan traveler who came upon him was moved with compassion when he saw him. He went up and bandaged his wounds, pouring oil and wine on them. He then lifted him on to his own mount, carried him to the inn and looked after him. Next day he took out two denarii and handed them to the innkeeper. 'Look after him,' he said, 'and on my way back I will make good any extra expense you have.' Which of these three do you think proved himself a neighbor to the man who fell into the brigands' hands?" "The one who took pity on him," he replied. Jesus said to him, "Go and do the same yourself."

Luke 10:29-39

REFLECTION

We can call Jesus the Good Samaritan because of the compassion he showed to the sick in befriending them and curing their illnesses. The depth of his love can be seen in his patient acceptance of suffering and death. His example, therefore, condemns the never-get-involved Catholic, the mind-your-own-business Catholic, the never-do-anyone-any-harm Catholic.

Christianity is, to a great extent, centered about caring. That is, showing genuine concern for our fellowman. This in turn means being moved to compassion and translating such feelings into direct involvement and action. Unless we think and act in terms of the needs of others, Jesus will have nothing to do with us: "In so far as you neglected to do this to one of the least of these, you neglected to do it to me."

Sickness can be a time of loneliness when people are in particular need of human friendship. It can also be a time of great spiritual upheaval when people are faced with the most fundamental questions and often assailed by doubt or even despair. Sick people need us to tell them that their suffering has meaning and that death is not to be feared. The lay person cannot content himself by saying that this is the responsibility of the priest. Through the gift of sacramental life we all share in the priesthood of Christ which means that we share in the healing power of Christ. We bring healing to the minds and hearts of the sick through our sympathy and kindness and through sharing with them our hope and trust in God's goodness.

Spending time with the sick is not all giving. We can learn much from them. They are often outstanding examples of patience and Christian joy as they accept God's will without complaint or self-pity. Contact with the sick should deepen our faith, make us grateful for the gift of health and remind us of the futility of materialistic living.

RESPONSE

1. Have we special concern for the sick?
2. What is our attitude toward mental illness?
3. Do we inquire about the well-being of people we know to be ill?
4. Do we ever visit sick people?
5. Should we give practical assistance to the sick or their dependents?
6. Is there room for improvement in our attitude toward the sick?

7 Jesus Falls the Second Time

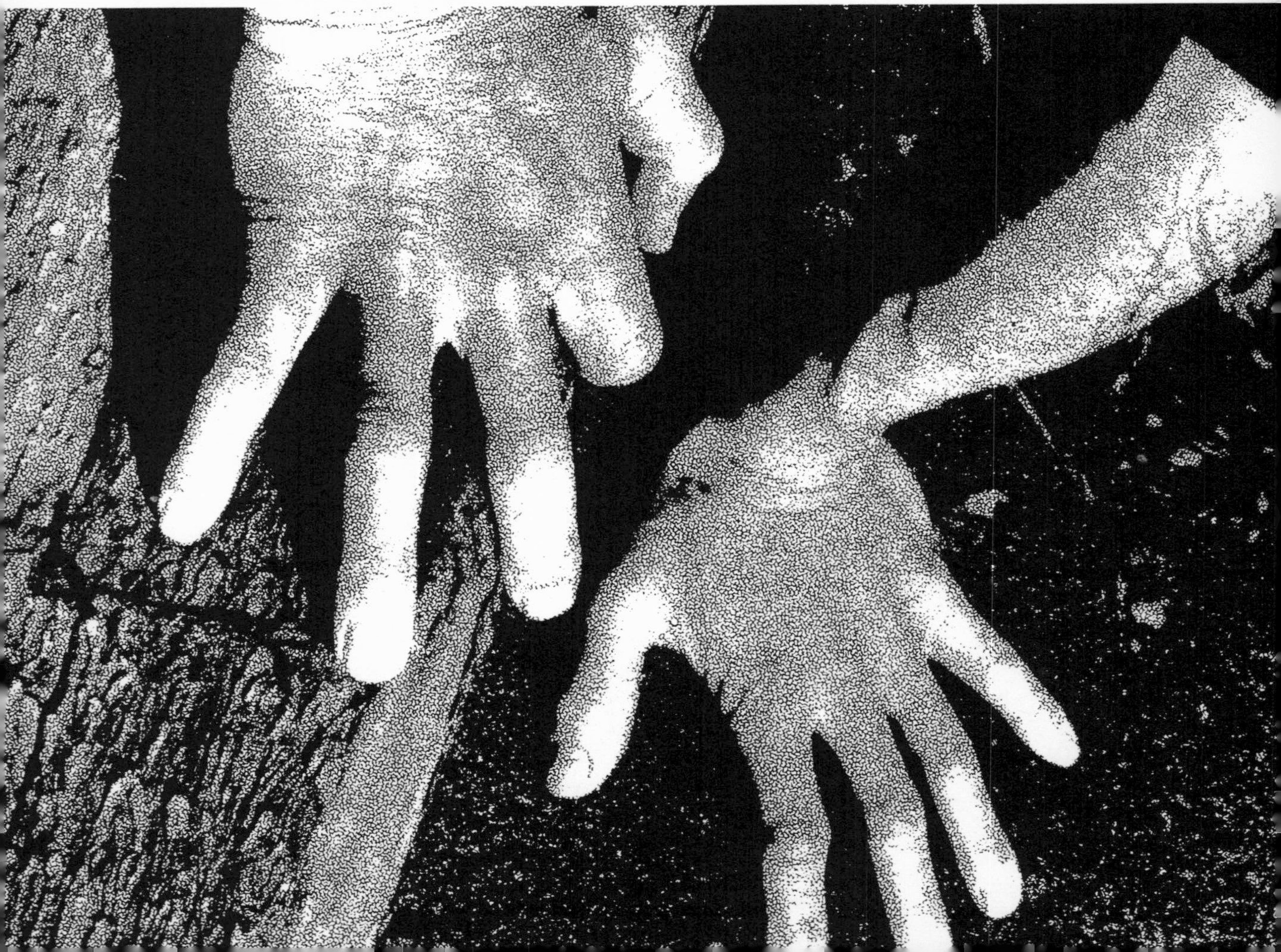

PRAYER

Lord, your way of the cross and your repeated falls remind
us of the certainty of death.

We are pilgrims and strangers on this earth journeying to
our homeland in heaven.

So often we forget that death is certain.

Help us to remember the shortness of this life and the eternity
of the next life.

Help us to keep before our minds your promise of eternal
life.

Lord, we are weak and selfish and we often fail to give
sympathy to the dying and the bereaved, and to attend
funerals.

Forgive us, Lord, for our many failures.

Send us the Holy Spirit, for left to ourselves we can do
nothing.

Lord, We can be so weak and helpless in the presence of the
dying and the bereaved.

Dear Jesus, help us to speak a comforting, uplifting word to
those who face death and their loved ones.

Help us to give them support and strength through our
sympathy. Send us your Holy Spirit, for
left to ourselves, we can do nothing

Carol

SUPPORT THE BEREAVED

Jesus demonstrates his love and his power over death.

Jesus went to a town called Nain, accompanied by his disciples and a great number of people. When he was near the gate of the town it happened that a dead man was being carried out for burial, the only son of his mother and she was a widow. And a considerable number of townspeople were with her. When the Lord saw her he felt sorry for her. "Do not cry," he said. Then he went up and put his hand on the bier and the bearers stood still, and he said, "Young man, I tell you to get up." And the dead man sat up and began to talk and Jesus gave him to his mother. Everyone was filled with awe and praised God saying, "A great prophet has appeared among us; God has visited his people."

Luke 7:11-17

Death should remind us that we are pilgrims on this earth; our real home is in heaven. The patience of Jesus should help us to wait patiently for the promise of heaven.

46

Carol

Carol

What we are waiting for is what Jesus promised: the new heavens and the new earth, the place where righteousness will be at home. So then, my friends, while you are waiting, do your best to live lives without spot or stain so that he will find you at peace. Think of our Lord's patience as your opportunity to be saved.

2 Peter 3:14-15

REFLECTION

The death of a friend or a loved one brings us face to face with the most fundamental questions in life. "Where is he now? Did his life have meaning or was it all wasted effort?" Death asks disturbing questions and they demand answers— now! The deepest longings of the human heart seek perfect order, peace and happiness. The believer knows that this perfection can be achieved only in heaven. The nonbeliever, however, tries to establish the kingdom of heaven on earth. In practice the Christian likes to have the best of both worlds. We want to accept Christ and his promises fully but the pleasures of life attract us. We can easily give in to the temptation of wanting our "heaven" now and so become preoccupied with trying to stay young, avoid pain and suffering, and get the maximum pleasure out of life. The more we have, the more the desire to have more snowballs. Luxuries become necessities and it gets increasingly hard to extricate ourselves from this life-style.

This way of life breeds an immunity to any serious consideration of death and its meaning. Failure to face up to the reality of death must account, in no small measure, for the level of stress, mental illness and suicide in Western civilization. Subconsciously, we all know that the only preparation for death is to lead a good life. Death disturbs us if our lives do not accord with the dictates of conscience, for we know that after death comes judgment when we shall have to give an account. Perhaps this is the reason why we avoid the dying and why so few attend funerals.

Death has meaning because Christ has overcome evil and death through his death and resurrection. That is why St. Paul could speak so positively about death. "At death, life is changed, not ended." "The sufferings of this life are not worthy to be compared with the glory that is to be revealed in us." We find Paul expressing even a longing for death. "To live in the body means to be exiled from the Lord." St. Francis was overjoyed at the prospect of death for he knew it meant union with the risen Lord in the happiness of heaven. "Welcome, sister death," he prayed.

The word "sympathy" means to suffer with, to identify, to feel what the other person is feeling. Jesus in us still wants to sympathize with the dying and the bereaved. It is a sad reflection on our Christianity if we do not give sympathy and support to the dying and bereaved. Death questions the depth of our faith and our acceptance of the glory promised by our Lord.

RESPONSE

1. What is our attitude toward the death of relatives, friends, our own death?
2. Do we ever think seriously about our own death?
3. Since death is certain, is it foolish not to think about it often?
4. If death makes us morbid or uneasy, what does this say about our faith?
5. Why should we be positive, and even happy, at the thought of death?

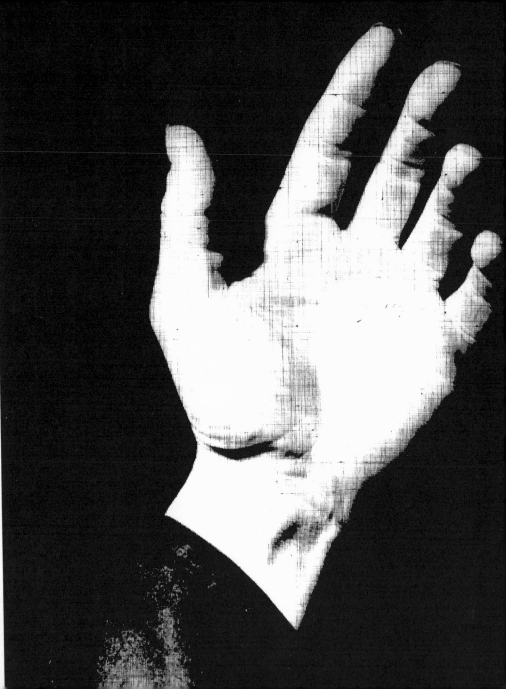

8 Jesus Meets the Women of Jerusalem

Lord, you said to the women of Jerusalem, "weep not for me, but for yourselves and for your children." Help us to see how destructive sin can be for individuals for families, and for the community of the baptized.

PRAYER

Lord, you tell us many times in the gospels of your love for
    sinners.
We cannot doubt the reality of your love as we see you
    carry your cross.
Lord, it was our sins that caused you such pain and suffering.
Make us truly sorry for our sins.
Give us the strength to turn away from everything evil in our
    lives.
Help us to accept the truth about ourselves when others point
    out our faults.
Dear Jesus, give us a deep love for the sinner.
Help us to take a sympathetic interest in the sinner.
Give us the courage to help him to turn away from sinful
    habits or practices.

---

carol

ADMONISH THE SINNER

Jesus reveals his Father's love for the sinner.

"Tell me. Suppose a man has a hundred sheep and one of them strays; will he not leave the ninety-nine on the hillside and go in search of the stray? I tell you solemnly, if he finds it, it gives him more joy than do the ninety-nine that did not stray at all. Similarly, it is never the will of your Father in heaven that one of these little ones should be lost."

Matthew 18:12-14

The unpleasant task of fraternal correction is a serious responsibility.

"If your brother does something wrong, go and have it out with him alone, between your two selves. If he listens to you, you have won back your brother. If he does not listen take one or two others along with you: the evidence of two or three witnesses is required to sustain any charge. But if he refuses to listen to these, report it to the community; and if he refuses to listen to the community, treat him like a pagan or a tax collector."

Matthew 18:15-17

Like Jesus, we must change people through our genuine interest.

While he was at dinner in the house it happened that a number of tax collectors and sinners came to sit at the table with Jesus and his disciples. When the pharisees saw this, they said to his disciples, "Why does your master eat with tax collectors and sinners?" When he heard this he replied, "It is not the healthy who need the doctor, but the sick. Go and learn the meaning of the words: What I want is mercy not sacrifice. And indeed I did not come to call the virtuous, but sinners."

Matthew 9:10-13

REFLECTION

Since we are all members of the Body of Christ there is no such thing as a private act or a purely personal act: every act has a social consequence. So if a man drinks too much, not only does he injure his own health, but he also injures the well-being of his wife and family. If he is a Christian he injures the wider family which is the Church.

One of the great tragedies of our time is that people are losing the sense of sin. In the newer societies there is a tendency to justify our wrong actions such as the jocular comment on petty theft. But sin has such destructive effects on the personal life of the individual, the family, and the community of the baptized that we must take seriously our Lord's command to the holy women: "Weep not for me but weep for yourselves and for your children."

53

Love demands that we take a deep, genuine interest in people. Jesus describes this love in the case of the man who looks for his stray sheep. But he demonstrates the unselfishness of love and its willingness to suffer alone in his meeting with the holy women as he carries his cross.

We meet so many human situations that cry out for our intervention, asking us to correct, admonish and give support. It could be the case of the father of a family whose drinking habits are a source of great pain and suffering to himself, his wife and his family. Or it may be a solo mother, pregnant and addicted to drugs, or a teenager who needs the advice of an interested person to correct his unwittingly selfish, irresponsible attitudes to life. There are so many situations where we can help. We must feel responsible. What can be more cruel, selfish and irresponsible, than to stand by and watch people do serious harm to themselves, their families and the Body of Christ?

It is important not to set ourselves up as judges. As well as accepting the responsibility to admonish the sinner, we must also be open to receive correction. The Book of Proverbs tells us that the wise man welcomes correction and expresses gratitude for it.

RESPONSE

1. Discuss the differences between responsible concern and self-righteous interference.
2. Do we use "not wanting to interfere" as an excuse for lack of interest in people?
3. What kind of relationship must we establish with a person before we can be in a position to correct him?
4. What positive approaches can we use to help people amend their ways?

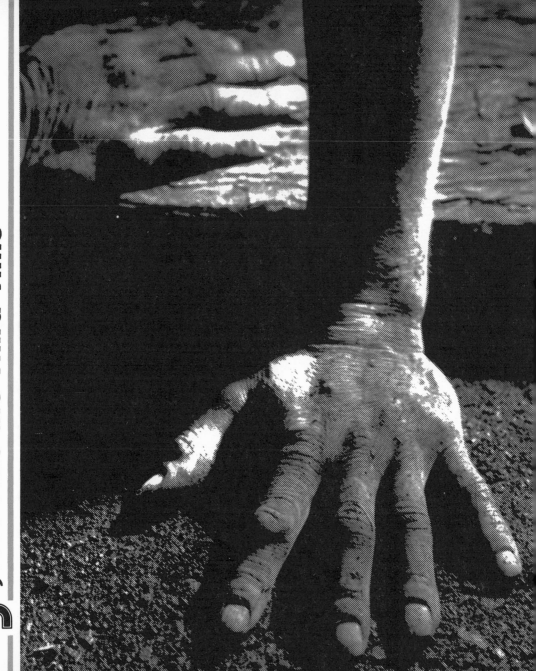

9 Jesus Falls the Third Time

PRAYER

O God, our Father, you display your infinite love for us in
    the agonizing death of your Son.
Enlighten our minds and hearts with a deep appreciation of
    our faith.
Help us to treasure it beyond all else.
Dear Jesus, our hearts go out to you as we see you fall a
    third time under the weight of the cross.
Forgive us our lack of effort in understanding the faith.
Forgive us our indifference in wanting to communicate the
    faith to others.
Dear Lord, break down the selfishness within us so that we
    can devote ourselves to the task of dispelling ignorance
    and spreading the Good News.
Send the Holy Spirit to fill us with enthusiasm that we may
    become true apostles, willing instruments in your hands.

Carol

SPREAD THE GOOD NEWS

Carol

Jesus calls us all to be his apostles.

Jesus came up and spoke to them. He said, "All authority in
heaven and on earth has been given to me. Go, therefore,
make disciples of all the nations; baptize them in the name of
the Father and of the Son and of the Holy Spirit, and teach
them to observe all the commands I gave you. And know
that I am with you always, yes to the end of time."

Matthew 28:18-20

**The evidence of our lives must point to the presence of
Jesus in the world.**

Jesus said, "No one lights a lamp and puts it in some hidden
place or under a tub, but on the lamp-stand so that people
may see the light when they come in. The lamp of your body
is your eye. When your eye is sound, your whole body too is
filled with light; but when it is diseased your body too will be
all darkness. If, therefore, your whole body is light inside

58

you and there is no trace of darkness, it will be light, entirely, as when the lamp shines out on yourself with its rays."

Luke 11:33-36

We must have courage enough to talk about our faith when the occasion demands it.

"If anyone declares himself for me in the presence of men, I will declare myself for him in the presence of my Father in heaven. But the one who disowns me in the presence of men, I will disown in the presence of my Father in heaven."

Matthew 10:32-33

REFLECTION

To be a Christian is to accept that we are one with Christ, Christ as risen Lord and Christ as we find him in our brothers and sisters. To accept Christ is also to accept what he said, adopting a certain set of values. St. Paul called it "putting on the mind of Christ." What does it mean to have the mind of Christ? The Father's will occupied Jesus fully when on earth and that will meant two things: worship of the Father and the salvation of all men. By word and example Jesus made the Father known to people who were ignorant of who the Father was. In this way Jesus offered people salvation, fulfillment, happiness, and taught them to offer worship to the Father in return for his love. To put on the mind of Christ, then, is to have his twofold concern: worship of the Father and the salvation of all men.

Jesus in us wants to reveal the reality of the Father's love to the great numbers of people who are ignorant of the Good News. The Good News is that the Father manifested his love when he sent his only son to die for us, raised him from the dead and sent the Holy Spirit to lead us to our home in heaven. To be convinced of all this and to know Jesus as a real friend in one's own experience is what Our Lord calls the pearl beyond price, the gift par excellence. St. Paul counted everything else as rubbish beside this gift, and the apostles said that the Good News meant so much to them that they could not promise to stop proclaiming it.

How much does the faith mean to us? Do we treasure it like St. Paul and the apostles? Jesus leaves us in no doubt as to our responsibility: "From whom much is given much is expected." He explains what he expects by telling us to be his apostles, a light and guide to people, living evidence of his presence in our lives. This means that we cannot limit the practice of our faith to Sunday Mass attendance and prayer. Jesus calls us all to be apostles in our own everyday situation. But before this is possible a deep appreciation of the faith is necessary and this comes from constant reading, reflection, discussion and prayer. Ignorance both in ourselves and in others is the one thing to overcome so that we can grow in the knowledge of God's love, put on the mind of Christ and be enthusiastic in wanting to spread the Good News.

What are the practical responsibilities of a Catholic?

1) Every Catholic should read the bible, especially the New Testament as well as Catholic papers and religious books. Discuss religious matters, pray in private and as a family.

Going to Mass should not be restricted to one day a week.

2) Be informed about the dangers of alcohol, drugs, gambling, dishonesty, abortion and try to influence people to adopt a more positive code of values.

3) Try to show people who live selfish lives that their selfishness makes them unhappy and that only love and a genuinely active concern for their less fortunate neighbor can set them free.

4) Be generous with your time by serving on committees, teaching Christian doctrine, working with youth, attending adult education classes, helping with parish projects.

5) Take a special interest in Catholics whose faith is weak, or who have given up the practice of their faith. Invite them to your home often and try to show them what a difference the faith could make in their lives.

6) Make the children of careless parents welcome in your home. Get them to join in family prayer and take them to Mass with you if they are Catholics.

7) Parents (the primary educators of their children) have a special responsibility to understand and appreciate the Good News so that they can communicate a joyful acceptance of it to their children.

By trying to understand the Christian message and live it out in our lives we give people a vision of the Father's kingdom which is a whole new way of looking at life. The sight of Jesus falling a third time under the weight of the cross reminds us of how much our faith cost Jesus, how much we should treasure it and how we should strive to communicate it to as many people as possible by our example and effort.

RESPONSE

1. Do we consider ourselves apostles?
2. What distinguishes us from the good neighbor who does not recognize God?

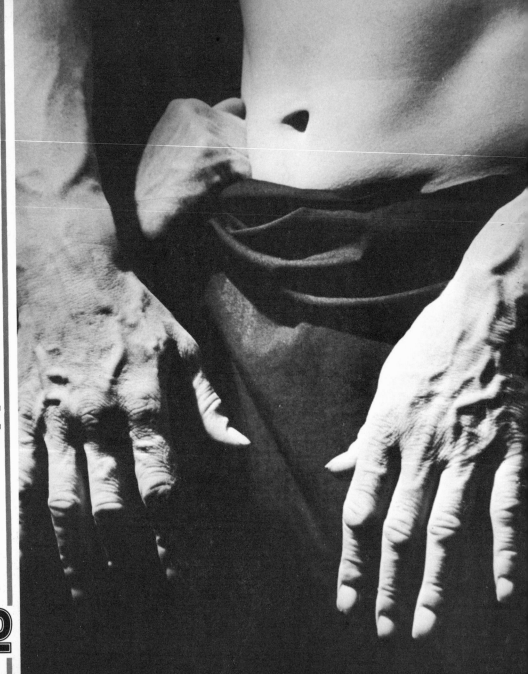

Lord Jesus, the sight of you stripped of your garments and accepting death out of love for all of humanity shows us the depth of your compassion. Let us remember to have compassion for the insecure, those with personal problems, and people who do not have faith in the reality of your love and mercy.

PRAYER

Lord, help us not to make false gods of material possessions.

Help us to see how the pleasures of this life have no
  permanence.

Purify us of pride, resentment, cynicism, prejudice and
  everything that weakens our faith.

Help us to take the time and the trouble to understand our
  faith more fully.

Strengthen our faith that we may not doubt your goodness in
  times of adversity.

Help us to be a support and a help to those who doubt your
  goodness and love.

Lord, we thank you for the many ways you demonstrate your
  love for us each day.

Our hearts are made for you and they can rest only when
  they rest in you.

Lord, thank you for the gift of faith, the pearl beyond price.

---

10. **Ann** *Jesus is stripped of his garments*

Carol

COUNSEL THE DOUBTFUL

Jesus dispels our doubts with his promise to be with us.

"Do not let your hearts be troubled.
Trust in God still, and trust in me.
There are many rooms in my Father's house;
If there were not I should have told you.
I am going now to prepare a place for you,
And after I have gone and prepared a place for you
I shall return to take you with me; so that where I am
    you may be too.
You know the way to the place where I am going."
Thomas said, "Lord, we do not know where you are going
    so how can we know the way?"
Jesus said: "I am the Way, the Truth and the Life, I will not
    leave you orphans; I will come back to you."

John 14:1-6, 18

**If we are like the pharisee, our pride keeps God at a
distance, but when we try to emulate the attitudes of the tax
collector, God reveals himself to us and our faith grows.**

66

Jesus spoke the following parable to some people who prided themselves on being virtuous and despised everyone else: "Two men went up to the Temple to pray, one a pharisee, the other a tax collector. The pharisee stood there and said this prayer to himself, 'I thank you God, that I am not grasping, unjust, adulterous, like the rest of mankind, and particularly that I am not like this tax collector here. I fast twice a week; I pay tithes on all I get.'

"The tax collector stood some distance away, not daring to raise his eyes to heaven; but he beat his breast and said, 'God, be merciful to me, a sinner.'

"This man, I tell you, went home again at rights with God; the other did not. For everyone who exalts himself will be humbled, but the man who humbles himself will be exalted."

Luke 18:9-14

REFLECTION

The human person is not capable of perfection. We are all subject to doubt and that is why no one can claim to have perfect faith. Doubt is an enemy we must resist for it can destroy our faith if we entertain it. Doubt can grow in us in many ways. The following may help us to deal with personal doubt and enable us to help others who are in doubt:

1) Our faith becomes subject to doubt if we place too much emphasis on material riches and pleasures. Our attention can become so centered on material things that there is little time left for God. This neglect of God in prayer,

reflection and worship is a very real cause of doubt.

2) Doubt about the faith can have deep underlying causes where a person lacks security and has a poor self-image. This is usually traceable to parental neglect in childhood. Before we can be secure and accept the idea of a loving God, we must first be convinced that at least one person loves us. If we do not experience this in childhood, we need to discover it from someone else later in life. We can all help the insecure person by taking a deep interest in him and by adopting a listening approach. If we are to be of any help, we must accept him wholeheartedly, making him feel he can speak without fear about himself and any feelings of deeds that may be troubling him. The solution to an insecure person's problems may depend largely on us and on the depth of our compassion. If we fail him, he may never find himself or God.

3) Doubts about God's goodness can often have emotional causes. We can help people by pointing out to them that their doubts come to the fore when they are depressed, unusually tense, or upset, which is to say that their doubts are caused by their moods or feelings.

4) Doubts can be caused by a poor or even wrong understanding of the faith where, for instance, a person's image of God might be one of fear. Before we can help, we ourselves need a true understanding of the faith.

5) Doubts can arise from selfish attitudes or habits and the

Lord will not reveal himself to us until we begin to live unselfishly. Advise the selfish person to become involved in trying to help others.

6) Unwillingness to forgive, lingering resentment, are an obvious sign of doubt in God's mercy. The guilt feelings that come from failure to forgive make a bad situation worse. Read the parables of God's mercy in Luke 15. Pray with the person and advise frequent confession where the healing power of our Lord's love can be experienced.

7) Admit to a person who feels doubt that you sometimes feel as he does. It is a source of strength to him to know that others are faced with similar problems. Share with him the ways in which you overcome your doubt. Point out the everyday signs of God's love—the gift of life, health, food, sleep, friendship and kindness of people.

8) Pride is a cause of doubt, making us think, like the pharisee, that we are the source of our own goodness. Pride makes us independent and prevents us from saying with the tax collector, "Lord, be merciful to me, a sinner."

9) Cynicism and prejudice do serious damage to our faith for they question God's goodness and kill our sense of wonder. It is important to cultivate the sense of wonder since it gives us a capacity for mystery and, therefore, makes it easier to accept God since God is full of mystery.

The sight of Jesus stripped of his garments and accepting death out of love for all mankind shows us the depth of his compassion. His example is a reminder to us to have compassion for the insecure, those with personal problems and those who doubt the reality of God's love and mercy. It is important that we realize that faith is God's free gift, infused by him, and not something we can manufacture for ourselves and for others. Our part is to be instruments, preparing the way for the Lord by removing the obstacles that prevent faith in ourselves and in others.

RESPONSE

1. Are our doubts of our own making?
2. How do we deal with doubts?
3. How should we deal with doubts in the light of the above readings?

Jesus Is Nailed to the Cross

PRAYER

Lord, make us instruments of your peace.
Where there is sadness make us bring joy.
Where there is loneliness make us bring comfort through
companionship.
Dear Jesus, we mourn as we reflect on what you suffered
for us.
And we mourn still more as we see you suffer in the lonely.
Forgive us for being blind to the pain of the lonely and for
lacking compassion.
Lord, we thank you for sharing your gift of peace with us.
Help us to show our gratitude in our efforts to share that
peace with the lonely.

Jesus is Nailed to the Cross

Carol

COMFORT THE LONELY

The great concern of Jesus was to share his peace with us, and thus to bring comfort to our lonely hearts.

Carol

"Peace I bequeath to you, my own peace I give you, a peace
 the world cannot give, this is my gift to you.
Do not let your hearts be troubled or afraid.
You heard me say:
I am going away, and shall return."

John 14:27-28

In his appearances after the resurrection, Jesus always greeted the apostles with, "Peace be with you" and left us the sacrament of Reconciliation before his departure.

Jesus came and stood among them. He said to them, "Peace be with you," and showed them his hands and his side. The disciples were filled with joy when they saw the Lord, and he said to them again, "Peace be with you. As the Father sent me, so am I sending you." After saying this he breathed on them and said: "Receive the Holy Spirit, for those whose sins you forgive, they are forgiven; for those whose sins you retain, they are retained."

John 20:20-23

The following passage from the prophet Isaiah foretells how Jesus was alone and abandoned during his passion and death. The passage could also be a description of a person deprived of companionship and the warmth of friendship.

74

The reading is a warning to us not to neglect the lonely and the mournful, but to recognize the suffering Jesus in each of them and his need for comfort.

Without beauty, without majesty we saw him, no looks to
    attract our eyes;
a thing despised and rejected by men, a man of sorrows and
    familiar with suffering, a man to make people screen
    their faces;
he was despised and we took no account of him.
On him lies a punishment that brings us peace, and through
    his wounds we are healed.

                                    Isaiah 53:2-3, 5

REFLECTION

Loneliness is one of the greatest problems of our time and is no respecter of persons. The rich are particularly prone to loneliness but the poor do not escape either. The old are lonely but young people are also lonely. Even those who appear to be happily married are often lonely. Why are people lonely? It is in part due to the fact that we do not belong on this earth. The song reminds us that "man is lonely by birth, man is only a pilgrim on earth." Man's loneliness is further added to by the conditions of modern living. But perhaps the most important contributing factor is our selfishness. We are insensitive, impersonal, uncaring. We take people for granted and, sad to say, this happens in what appear to be happy homes.

What the world needs most is the kind of love that caused Jesus to accept death as humbly as a lamb. His love was so great that he identified totally with us, taking upon himself all our pain and suffering, sharing in all our loneliness and grief. It is this kind of empathy that we must want to show to every person, trying to feel what they feel, trying to share in the pain of their situation.

Loneliness is the root cause of many problems. Because we are social beings one of our deepest needs is to communicate. Failure to do so brings isolation, estrangement and loneliness. Loveless marriages, unhappy homes, unhappy people, show how little real communication is done. The guts of communication is listening. The world is full of lonely people who want to pour out their worries and troubles but so few are interested enough to listen. We, who receive the peace of Christ, should want to share that peace with others. One of the most important ways in which we can do this is to have empathy with people, providing them with a listening ear.

We may need to ask ourselves some basic questions. Are we domineering or superior in our attitude to people? Do we want to do all the talking? Can we resist giving people advice? Do people feel at home in our presence? Advice costs nothing and helps little. What the lonely are looking for is compassion, a friend who cares enough to want to listen. Perhaps a person is uncommunicative because we have lacked sensitivity and interest when they tried to communicate, and consequently they have given up the effort. Our task then is to recognize that Jesus is lonely in every person, even in those closest to us, and recognizing this, try to do everything we can to create an atmosphere where every person feels at home in our presence, free to talk about himself and his problems. If we are compassionate they will be willing to accept our advice.

Charity begins at home but does not end there. Jesus in us wants to reach so many with his peace. We must replace the selfish, independent, man-mind-thyself attitude with the neighborly, homely attitude. A woman said of a troublesome child, "I used to chase him, but one day I took him home and found out the family's difficulties." Make a point of getting to know your ten nearest neighbors. Invite old people or lonely people to a meal.

"Greater love no man has than he lay down his life for his friends." Jesus, submitting to his death, teaches us how we must lay down our lives by our willingness to be a friend to every person. He teaches us to combat loneliness by building up neighborliness and by making people feel wanted.

RESPONSE

1. How should the scripture readings affect us?
2. What does it mean to be hospitable?
3. Are we hospitable?
4. Should we ever invite an old person or a lonely person to a meal?
5. Do we care enough to spend time with someone who is lonely?

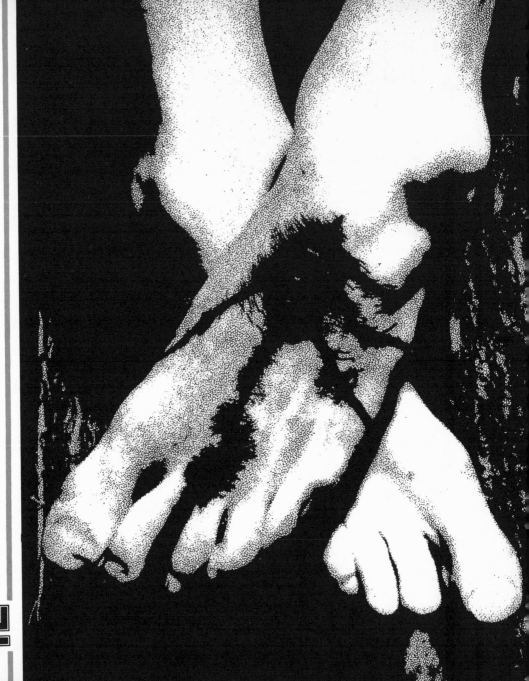

PRAYER

My Jesus, I look at you hanging from the cross and think:
Am I worth this much?
What can I give you in return?
Lord, I will try to accept whatever suffering life brings.
Give me the strength to forgive.
Help me to see people as ignorant rather than cruel, in need
    of love and forgiveness rather than chastisement.
Jesus, gentle and humble of heart,
Give me a heart like yours.

12 Ann Jesus dies on the cross

Carol

BEAR WRONGS PATIENTLY

Our willingness to bear wrongs patiently shows the depth of our faith.

"You have learnt how it was said: You must love your neighbor and hate your enemy. But I say to you: Love your enemies and pray for those who persecute you; in this way you will be sons of your Father in heaven, for he causes his sun to rise on bad men as well as on good and his rain to fall on honest and dishonest men alike. For if you love those who love you, what right have you to claim any credit? Even tax collectors do as much, do they not? And if you save your greetings for your brothers, are you doing anything exceptional? Even the pagans do as much, do they not? You must therefore be perfect just as your heavenly Father is perfect."

Matthew 5:43-48

Jesus, dying on the cross, teaches us never to become bitter. Instead, we must pray for our enemies. "Father, forgive them for they know not what they do."

80

Always be wanting peace with all people and the holiness without which no one can ever see the Lord. Be careful that no one is deprived of the grace of God and that no root of bitterness should begin to grow and make trouble; this can poison a whole community.

Hebrews 12:14-15

The death of Jesus has overcome the powers of evil. This gives us confidence to share in the vision of Isaiah which sees the universal reign of peace.

"The wolf lives with the lamb, the panther lies down with the
    kid, calf and lion cub feed together with a little boy to
    lead them. . . .
The lion eats straw like the ox.
The infant plays over the cobra's hole; into the viper's lair
    the young child puts his hand."

Isaiah 11:6-8

REFLECTION

The weapons Jesus chose to spread his revolution of love were meekness and humility. He chose to combat hatred and violence by meekness rather than by force. This is why Jesus applied the Messianic prophecies to himself, prophecies in which he is presented as gentle and humble. "He will not wrangle or cry aloud, nor will anyone hear his voice in the streets." His meekness, unpretentiousness and humility are further emphasized in the image of the lamb accepting death without complaint.

Gandhi and Martin Luther King believed in meekness not only for themselves but for everyone. They saw meekness as an instrument of individual peace as well as an instrument of universal liberation. St. Francis of Assisi, bearing the wounds of Christ in his hands and feet, is the epitome of meekness. In his prayer he begs the Lord for meekness so as to be an instrument of his peace: "Where there is hatred let me sow love."

How well do we succeed in being meek? The many wars which Christians support so enthusiastically show how this beatitude is neglected. We have two ways of reacting to wrongs, insults, injuries. The first choice is to "stand up for yourself" by repaying violence with violence, insult with insult, evil with evil. To choose this course is to nurse and intensify hatred and resentment. This not only destroys our own individual peace but it also closes the door to the possibility of reconciliation and peace. But we have another, more difficult choice. That is to recognize in that hurt or insult the sin of the world in which we all share and to recognize in it, too, the person of Christ hanging from the cross, defiled by scourgings, belittled by insults. It is easy to take revenge but difficult to love—we must love. We must see people as ignorant rather than cruel, in need of love and forgiveness rather than chastisement.

A story is told of a follower of Martin Luther King giving advice to a Negro boy who was assaulted by a white man for frequenting a toilet reserved for white people. "You have two choices," he said to the boy. "The first choice is to hurl a stone at your enemy, run home, and let your anger and resentment fester and intensify as you relive your experience with your family and friends. You must follow the second course of action because it alone will bring peace and well-being. Forgive your enemy in the name of Jesus. Try to see him as more ignorant than cruel. The only way in which we can build society is through the power of meekness and forgiveness."

Having the vision of Isaiah—the vision for which our Lord died—we must build up society with the power and violence of meekness. Happiness begins at the moment we overcome ourselves and pardon the brother who hurts us.

RESPONSE

1. Do we accept Jesus at his word in the first scripture reading above?
2. Are we willing to make sacrifices and even to suffer in the interests of peace and harmony?
3. When ought we to imitate the meekness of Jesus?

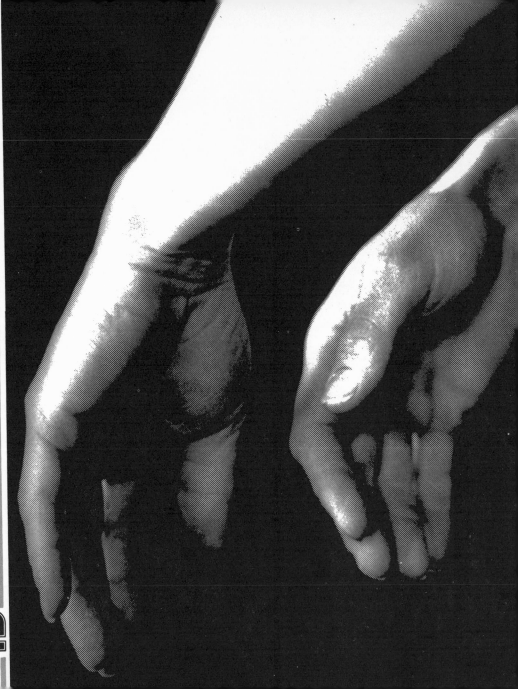

PRAYER

Thank you Lord for having suffered so much for us.
Thank you for forgiving us again and again for our many
   crimes.
We find it so hard to forgive, Lord,
And to be able to forgive is a special gift from you.
Lord, we are unworthy of your love.
Through the merits of your passion and death give us the
   strength to overcome all hatred, resentment and
   bitterness.
Fill our hearts with mercy and compassion.
Make us all willing instruments of your peace.

FORGIVE ALL INJURIES

Carol →

**The following parable should soften our hardheartedness
if we find it hard to forgive others, especially when we
consider the suffering our sins caused Jesus.**

"And so the kingdom of heaven may be compared to a
King who decided to settle his accounts with his servants.
When the reckoning began they brought him a man who
owed ten thousand talents; but he had no means of paying,
so his master gave orders that he should be sold together
with his wife and children and all his possessions to meet the
debt. At this, the servant threw himself down at the master's
feet. "Give me time," he said, "and I will pay the whole
sum." And the servant's master felt so sorry for him that he
let him go and cancelled the debt. Now as the servant went
out, he happened to meet a fellow servant who owed him
one hundred denarii and he seized him by the throat and
began to throttle him. "Pay what you owe me," he said. His
fellow servant fell at his feet and implored him saying, "Give
me time and I will pay you." But the other would not agree;
on the contrary, he had him thrown into prison until he
should pay the debt. His fellow servants were deeply
distressed when they saw what had happened and they went
to their master and reported the whole affair to him. Then
the master sent for him. "You wicked servant," he said.
"I cancelled all the debt of yours when you appealed to me.
Were you not bound then to have pity on your fellow servant
just as I had pity on you?" And in his anger the master

86

handed him over to the torturers till he should pay all his debts. And that is how my heavenly Father will deal with you unless you each forgive your brother from your heart."

Matthew 18:23-35

We can place no limit on the extent of our forgiveness.

Then Peter went up to him and said, "Lord, how often must I forgive my brother if he wrongs me? As often as seven?" Jesus answered, "Not seven, I tell you, but seventy-seven times."

Matthew 18:21-22

We can expect to receive only to the extent that we are generous in giving.

"Be compassionate as your Father is compassionate. Do not judge, and you will not be judged yourselves; do not condemn and you will not be condemned yourselves; grant pardon, and you will be pardoned, give and there will be gifts for you, a full measure pressed down, shaken together and running over, will be poured into your lap; because the amount you measure out is the amount you will be given back."

Luke 6:36-38

REFLECTION

The God-man battered, broken, dead. Why? His love accepted it all because he wanted to overcome the powers of evil: hatred, bitterness, resentment, everything that keeps man unhappy and enslaved. His dying was a giant act of love that said: "I forgive you all totally and completely. Please accept my forgiveness by forgiving yourselves and by forgiving each other."

Our personal peace depends on whether we accept our Lord's forgiveness. As we learn to appreciate his mercy, we learn to be gentle with ourselves and to forgive ourselves. But it is also necessary to forgive others since we can have no peace while entertaining bitterness or resentment.

If we fail to forgive, bitterness can grow to the point of making us mentally ill. That is why it is imperative to forgive everyone from our hearts. Not to do so is to be guilty of a serious act of violence toward oneself which may amount to suicide. If we forgive, we experience freedom, joy, peace, happiness.

Parents have a special responsibility to teach their children to forgive. Unless children see their parents asking pardon of each other and of their children, children will grow up with the philosophy of an eye for an eye. We all need to be on our guard against subtle forms of resentment which we express in cynical, sarcastic or belittling ways, or by cold silence. Jesus died to bring home to us how essential forgiveness is to our well-being.

By performing miracles, Jesus brought healing to people, not only physical healing but also healing of mind and heart. He brought healing to Peter after the triple denial with a silent look. Jesus still wants to bring his healing action to sinners through our forgiving hearts. Our great task is to be the instruments of the peace of Jesus and one of the greatest ways of mediating this peace is through forgiveness. When people know we forgive them we win their admiration and respect and open their eyes to the power of God's love. This will help people more than all the self-righteous advice we can give them.

We find it hard to forgive people because we quickly lose sight of the battered body of Jesus, crushed by our sins. We are also too quick to judge people and to blame them for the way they behave. Our superficial approach to people does not look beyond surface appearances to the deeper image of Christ in every person. We need to try to understand people's problems by giving some thought to the reason why they behave as they do and these reasons are often beyond their control. The parable of the unjust steward and the broken corpse of Jesus show how much we have been forgiven and how much we need to forgive in turn. Constant awareness of the sufferings of Jesus gives us the strength to forgive. Frequent confession is also a source of great strength.

RESPONSE

1. Do you regard yourself as guilty of the murder of Jesus?
2. Why do we sometimes find it hard to forgive?
3. Why is forgiveness so necessary?

14 Jesus Is Laid in the Tomb

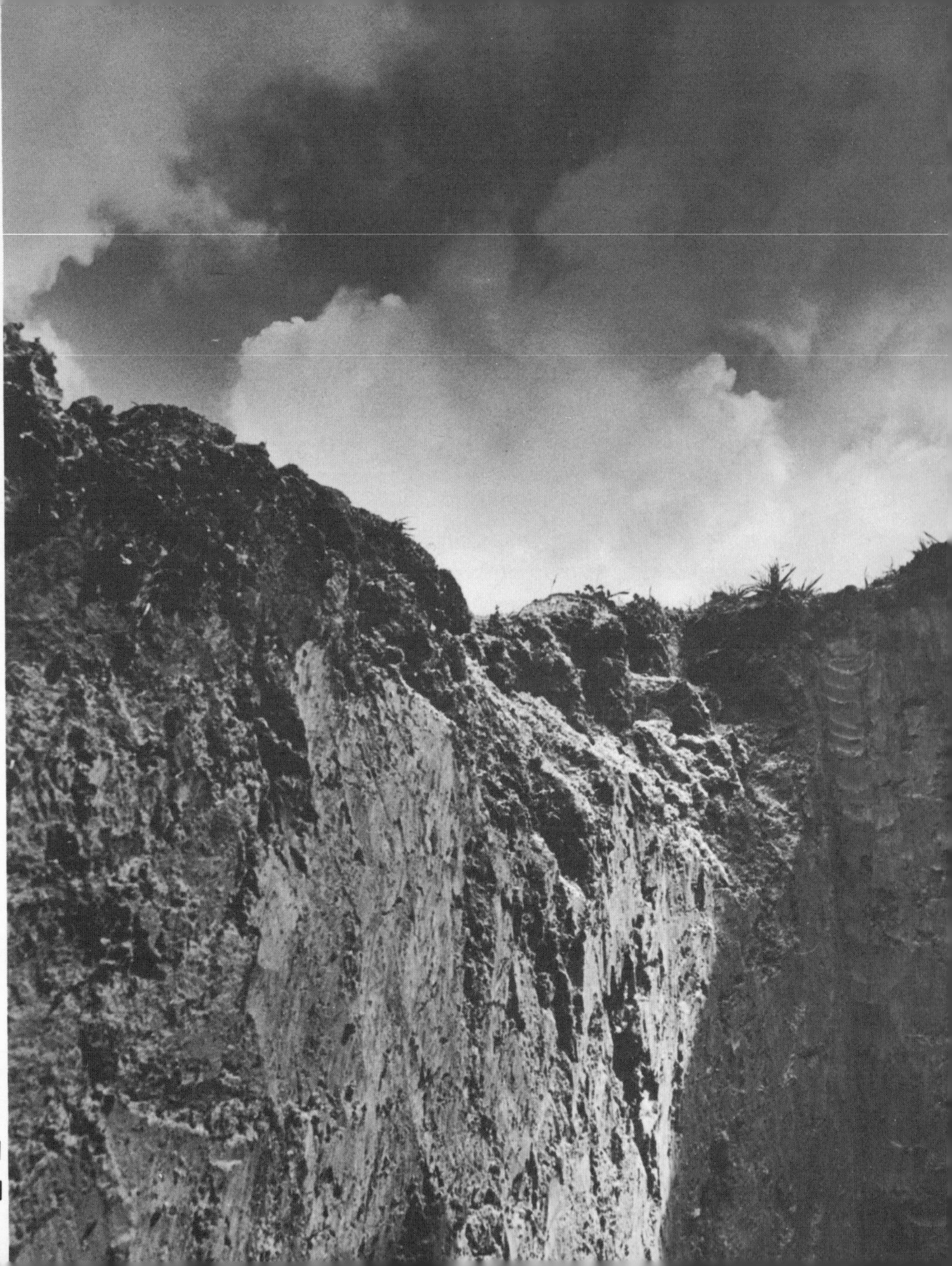

PRAYER

Father, thank you for creating us in your own image and
    likeness.
You did not abandon us when we turned away from you in
    sin.
You so loved us as to send your only Son.
Thank you, Jesus, for undertaking such suffering for us.
Thank you for the peace you share with us through your
    death and resurrection.
Thank you for the gift of the Holy Spirit.
Through his power help us to live only for you, to share the
    concern of your heart, and to offer our lives in your
    service, for the salvation of all men. *people.*

14. *Jesus is Laid in the Tomb*

Carol →

PRAY FOR THE LIVING AND THE DEAD

We must not cut ourselves off from God like the prodigal son, living selfish lives. We belong to Christ and therefore we must live for him, in accordance with his will.

You are not your own property; you have been bought and paid for. That is why you should use your body for the glory of God.

1 Corinthians 6-20

None of us lives for himself only, none of us dies for himself only; if we live, it is for the Lord that we live, and if we die, it is for the Lord that we die. Whether we live or die, then, we belong to the Lord. For Christ died and rose to life in order to be the Lord of the living and the dead.

Romans 14:7-9

Jesus commands us to pray with confidence and trust.

"Ask, and it will be given to you; search, and you will find; knock, and the door will be opened to you. For the one who asks always receives; the one who searches always finds; the one who knocks always will have the door opened to him. Is there a man among you who would hand his son a stone when he asked for bread? Or would hand him a snake when he asked for a fish? If you, then, who are evil, know how to give your children what is good, how much more will your Father in heaven give good things to those who ask him!"

Matthew 7:7-11

The importance of silence can be seen in this admonition of Jesus.

"In your prayers do not babble as the pagans do, for they think that by using many words they will make themselves heard. Do not be like them; your Father knows what you need before you ask him."

Matthew 6:7-9

REFLECTION

To use our time and talents in the service of others is not the only grace God gives us: we also have the grace of prayer. Prayer is an awesome experience since it consists of stepping into the presence of the all-holy God.

Prayer, in contrast to good works, is not something we do. It is the transforming action of the Holy Spirit in us when we surrender to him and allow him to work in us. Our lives have

93

value only insofar as we allow the Holy Spirit to sanctify us. So too, our prayers for others.

This approach shows the need to practice silence in our periods of prayer, thus to wait patiently on the Lord, listen to the inspirations of the Holy Spirit, and offer the Father the praise and adoration of our hearts. Prayer, then, is not just a matter of going out to God, addressing oneself to God or raising one's mind and heart to him. This kind of prayer has its place, but silent surrender of one's heart to Jesus is of much greater importance. Jesus speaks to us in silence when we are obedient to the command of the psalm: "Be still and know that I am God." That is to say: "Be silent and still. Acknowledge your total dependence on me. Have faith in me. I am God, infinite and almighty. But I am also love. I want to befriend you. I want to invade your whole being with my healing light—if you will allow me." Prayer is the greatest power the world knows for it is the power of God himself.

This power comes from being one with Jesus: "It is no longer I who live but Jesus lives in me." That is why we pray through Jesus, with Jesus and in Jesus.

Here a serious objection arises. How can busy people, immersed in so much activity, find time for prayer each day? The answer is simply to put first things first, as Jesus reminds us: "Seek first the kingdom of God and all other things will be added to you." Every person has a most serious responsibility to himself, to others, and to God to make time for prayer.

The value of prayer can be seen in the face of a Mother Teresa or a Padre Pio as they radiate God's heavenly peace, a peace the world cannot give. This shows that the death of Christ has not been in vain. He still lives to transform us with his healing light so that we can be truly happy and be Christ to others.

RESPONSE

1. Who are you?
2. Is life worth living?
3. What is your destiny?
4. Do you ever feel that God has deserted you?
5. Should you feel guilty if you lose heart and stop trying?
6. To what extent does prayer depend on you?